AFTMA'S POCKET GUIDE TO
FISHING INSHORE SALT WATER

FM Publishing, Inc.

Phoenix, Md.

Distributed exclusively to the book trade by
Stackpole Books, Cameron &
Kelker Streets, P.O. Box 1831,
Harrisburg, PA 17105 1-800-READ-NOW.

Special thanks to A.F.T.M.A. for their help in preparing this edition. Also, thanks to Mark Susinno, a young artist who is long on talent and quick on the uptake.

**Cover Painting by
Mark Susinno**

ILLUSTRATION AND PHOTO CREDITS

AFTMA- 18,19; Pete Barrett-36; Berkley & Co.-13,14,17; Burgess Blevins-1; Bill Burton-20,38,40,52,54,60,67,74, 86,88; Cary de Russy-6,40; Eagle Electronics-47; Louis Frisno-22,23,24; Larry Horseman-54; Lefty Kreh-73; Rob Merz-28,30,31,32; O. Mustad-8; National Park Service-66; PA Fish Com.-28; J.F. Pepper Co.-73; Boyd Pfeiffer-38,43,56; Sampo, Inc.-8; Henry Schaefer-77; Somerville Art Studios-9,10,11; Mark Susinno-Cover, 24,25,26,27, 32,33,34,62,64,69,72,76,78,79; Russ Wilson-70; Zebco Corp-16,17.

Published by FIM Publishing, Inc.
P.O. Box 197, Phoenix, MD 21131

Printed in the United States of America

Pocket Guide to Fishing Series
ISBN   0-917131-00-2
Inshore Salt Water
ISBN   0-917131-03-7

To Our Young Readers

If you're into drugs or alcohol, chances are this book won't do you much good. It's not that you won't learn something-you will. But, if your head isn't clear, you will miss the tranquility of a lake at sunrise, the serenity of a clear mountain stream, not to mention the delicate strike of a fish on the end of your line. It's really very simple, fishing provides its own natural high! No need for some mind altering drug. Besides, fishing under the influence of drugs or alcohol can be very dangerous.

Some people say that youngsters, or for that matter adults, take drugs to forget their problems. If you think this is the case, forget it! Your problems will still be there when you sober up, along with possibly a new one- drug dependency.

A lot of adults don't know how to fish. If you have never been, chances are the people raising you fall into this category. Why don't you suggest to them that you all learn together. Funny thing about fishing-with a little instruction, which this book will provide, anyone can be successful. You learn as you do it. You also get away from this hectic world we live in and get a chance to really relax. It's a great way to get to know someone, like the people who are trying to raise you.

Marcel C. Malfregeot Jr.
Administrative Assistant
Harrison County Schools
Clarksburg, WV

CONTENTS

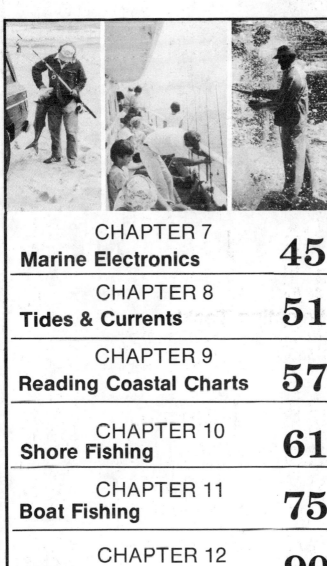

6

1
SELECTING TACKLE

Saltwater fishing requires heavier tackle than that used on rivers and reservoirs. Not only are the species being sought larger, but a new element must be taken into consideration-the tides. There is no such thing as a rod and reel combination that does it all. Ranging from rigs using 10 to 12 pound test line for brackish water largemouth bass, to wire line used in many areas of the country to troll for toothy battlers like bluefish, the length and action of your rod can range from 6′ medium action to 15′ rods used by some surf anglers.

Although there are those who specialize in fly fishing for such species as bonefish, and others who prefer baitcasting equipment for bass, the average angler will normally choose a heavier version of open faced spinning reel in combination with a 6′ to 7′ rod designed to handle lines in the 14 to 20 pound test catagory.

Most shore fishing in tidal waters is done from fishing piers, bridges and the surf. Although there are variations on the rigs you will use, the standard bottom rig with a variety of different sinkers will cover most situations.

When selecting the rod and reel combination for your fishing activities, it is important that the rod, reel and pound test line you select be designed to work with each other. Known as **BALANCED TACKLE**, your selection should also take into consideration the kind of fishing

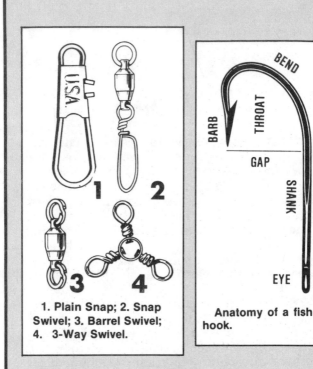

1. Plain Snap; 2. Snap Swivel; 3. Barrel Swivel; 4. 3-Way Swivel.

Anatomy of a fish hook.

and the weight of the rigs you will be using. If most of your angling endeavors will revolve around bottom fishing with heavy sinkers, you wouldn't want to buy a rod and reel combination that was too light to handle this **terminal tackle**.

Monofilament fishing line is the most popular line in use today. It is made from nylon and graded into **pound test catagories**. Ideally, 12 pound test line will break if you pick up a

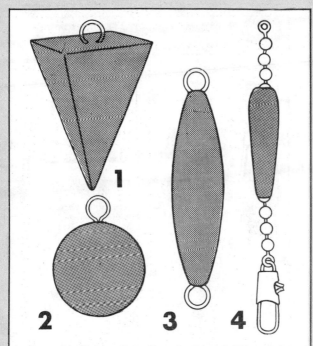

1. **Pyramid Sinker:** Excellent bottom fishing and surf fishing sinker; 2. **Cushion Sinker:** Good drift fishing sinker; 3. **In-Line Sinker:** Used in some trolling rigs; 4. **Bead Chain Sinker:** Used in trolling and some casting.

weight that weighs more than 12 pounds.

Hooks come in all shapes and sizes. For most saltwater fishing you will be using the larger series. This group is graded with a /0 after the appropriate size number. Beginning with 1/0, the smallest, the series goes up to 14/0 which is used offshore for large game fish.

The sinkers you will use with live bait will normally not be much smaller than 1 ounce. Their main purpose is to get your offer-

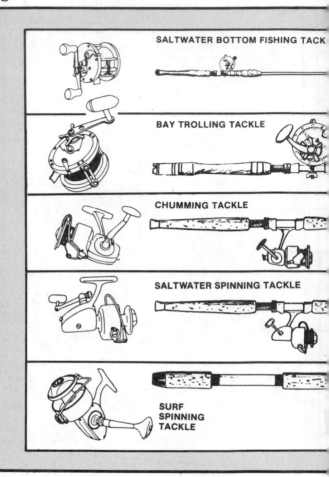

SALTWATER BOTTOM FISHING TACK

BAY TROLLING TACKLE

CHUMMING TACKLE

SALTWATER SPINNING TACKLE

SURF SPINNING TACKLE

ing to the bottom and apply enough tension on your fishing line so you can feel the fish strike.

Swivels are devices used to attach lures and other terminal tackle to your line or prevent twisting. The plain snap is used when fishing an artificial lure. The snap swivel is normally used in any fishing situation that requires a bottom rig, and the barrel swivel is most often used in trolling rigs. The three-way swivel may be part of your bottom rig.

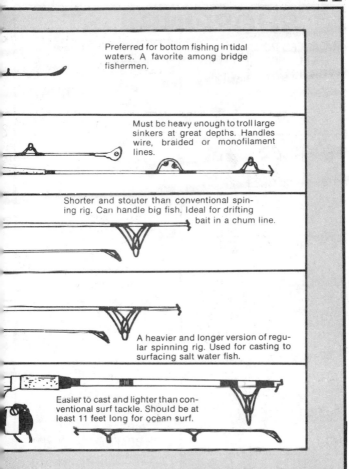

Preferred for bottom fishing in tidal waters. A favorite among bridge fishermen.

Must be heavy enough to troll large sinkers at great depths. Handles wire, braided or monofilament lines.

Shorter and stouter than conventional spinning rig. Can handle big fish. Ideal for drifting bait in a chum line.

A heavier and longer version of regular spinning rig. Used for casting to surfacing salt water fish.

Easier to cast and lighter than conventional surf tackle. Should be at least 11 feet long for ocean surf.

Bobbers may also be used in salt water. These devices are attached to your line to hold your rig at a certain depth and signal when you have a strike. Obviously, since your rig is much heavier in salt water, the bobbers you choose should be bigger.

It is important to remember that salt water is very corrosive. Always wash your rod and reel in fresh water after you have been fishing. A few minutes with a hose will do the job.

SHOPPING LIST

BALANCED ROD, REEL AND FISHING LINE

LAKES & RIVERS
5½' - 7' rod with 6 lb. to 14 lb. line

SALT WATER
6' - 7' rod with 14 lb. to 20 lb. line

TACKLE BOX Big Enough for Additional Tackle

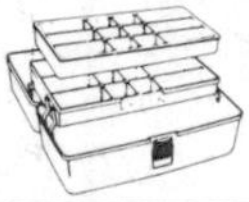

LAKES & RIVERS
SALT WATER
Make sure it is worm proof.

BAIT BUCKET

Useful in fresh & salt water. Keeps live bait, like minnows alive.

SWIVELS Packages of Each

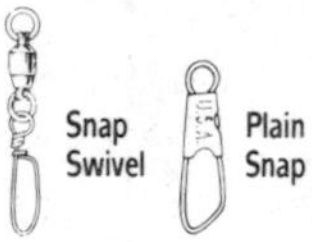

LAKES & RIVERS
Sizes #12 - #10 Plain Snap for lures; Snap Swivel for bottom rigs.

SALT WATER
Sizes #7, #1, 1/0 snap swivels for bottom rigs.

SINKERS Assorted Packs

LAKES & RIVERS
Split Shot or Pinch On ¼ oz. - ¾ oz.
Bank Sinker Kind ⅛ oz. - ¾ oz.

SALT WATER
Split Shot or Pinch On ½ oz. - 1 oz.
Bank & Pyramid 1 oz. - 4 oz.

HOOKS Pack of Assorted Pack of Snelled

LAKES & RIVERS
Pack of plain hooks #8 - #2, 2/0
Pack of Snelled for bottom rig. Sizes #8 - #2, 2/0

SALT WATER
Snelled, Sizes 1/0 - 5/0 with wire leader.

LINE CLIPPERS

Always good to have for snipping off excess line.

GOOD KNIFE

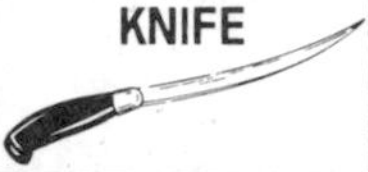

Good for cutting live bait and filleting catch.

BOBBERS 3 Different Sizes

Normally used with bottom rigs. Match up with sinker sizes.

BOTTOM RIGS (3)

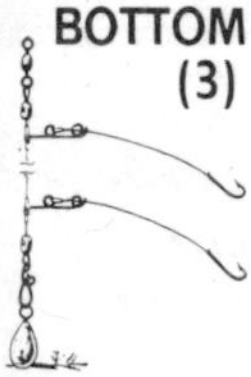

LAKES & RIVERS
Usually called Crappie Rigs. Normally comes with hooks.

SALT WATER
Usually called Top & Bottom Rigs. Should have wire leader.

NEEDLE NOSE PLIERS

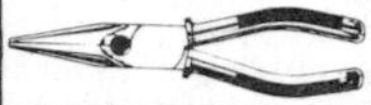

Has many uses. Good for removing hooks and lures from fish's mouth.

STRINGER OR BUCKET

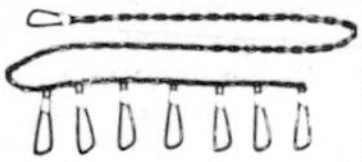

LAKES & RIVERS
Either

SALT WATER
Bucket

ARTIFICIAL LURES

LAKES & RIVERS
1) Single Shaft Spinner
2) Plastic Worms, Sizes 6"-8" with 1/0-4/0 Worm Hooks and ⅛ - ⅝ Slip Sinkers.
3) (1 each) ¼-⅜ oz. Surface Lure, Medium Diver & Deep Diver.

SALT WATER
Mainly used in trolling from boat.

2
KNOTS

The knot is the weakest point in your fishing line and one of the main reasons for fish getting away. It makes sense that you should tie the strongest most reliable knot you can.

The knots demonstrated on this page and the next should cover most situations you might encounter. In the next chapter we will go into the proper casting techniques. It will be suggested to you that casting requires a lot of practice that should take place before you go fishing. It is also a good idea to become as familiar as you can with the knots that can make or break a fishing trip.

Arbor Knot
The Arbor Knot provides the angler with a quick, easy connection for attaching line to the reel spool.

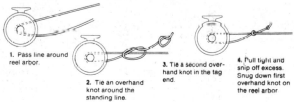

1. Pass line around reel arbor.

2. Tie an overhand knot around the standing line.

3. Tie a second overhand knot in the tag end.

4. Pull tight and snip off excess. Snug down first overhand knot on the reel arbor

Improved Blood Knot
The Improved Blood Knot is used for tying two pieces of monofilament together of relatively equal diameters.

1. Overlap the ends of your two strands that are to be joined and twist them together about 10 turns.

2. Separate one of the center twists and thrust the two ends through the space as illustrated.

3. Pull knot together and trim off the short ends.

14

Trilene® Knot

The Trilene Knot is a strong, reliable connection that resists slippage and premature failures. It works best when used with Trilene premium monofilament fishing line.

The Trilene Knot is an all-purpose connection to be used in joining Trilene to swivels, snaps, hooks and artificial lures. The knot's unique design and ease of tying yield consistently strong, dependable connections while retaining 85-90% of the original line strength. The double wrap of mono through the eyelet provides a protective cushion for added safety.

1. Run end of line through eye of hook or lure and double back through the eye a second time.

2. Loop around standing part of line 5 or 6 times.

3. Thread tag end back between the eye and the coils as shown.

4. Pull up tight and trim tag end.

Palomar Knot

The Palomar Knot is a general-purpose connection used in joining monofilament to swivels, snaps, hooks and artificial lures. The double wrap of mono through the eyelet provides a protective cushion for added safety.

1. Double the line and form a loop three to four inches long. Pass the end of the loop through hook's eye.

2. Holding standing line between thumb and finger, grasp loop with free hand and form a simple overhand knot.

3. Pass hook through loop and draw line while guiding loop over top of eyelet.

4. Pull tag end of line to lighten knot snugly and trim tag end to about ⅛".

Double Surgeon's Loop

The Double Surgeon's Loop is a quick, easy way to tie a loop in the end of a leader. It is often used as part of a leader system because it is relatively strong.

1. Double the tag end of the line. Make a single overhand knot in the double line.

2. Hold the tag end and standing part of the line in your left hand and bring the loop around and insert through the overhand knot again.

3. Hold the loop in your right hand. Hold the tag end and standing line in your left hand. Moisten the knot (don't use saliva) and pull to tighten.

4. Trim off the tag end.

3
HOW TO USE YOUR ROD & REEL

Unless you choose to concentrate on brackish water bass fishing, chances are that most of your early saltwater fishing will not rely on accurate casting. However, you can never tell when you might come across fish feeding on the surface, when this talent will be called for. It's always a good idea to be thoroughly familar with your equipment and how it is used.

The instruction offered in this chapter is confined to the basic overhead cast with an open faced spinning reel and the basic surf cast. These techniques will cover most situations you will encounter, even though there are other casting techniques in use today. Also, bait casting equipment employs a system that is very different, due to the design of that equipment. What's important, be it casting an open faced spinning rod and reel, or giant surf fishing tackle, is being familar with your gear.

After you have reviewed the material on the following pages and mastered the basic overhead cast, it's time for a little target practice. Place several objects, such as towels or garbage can lids, at various distances and cast to them until you hit each consistently. Now, try moving back and forth from your targets. You will be amazed at how quickly you develop the necessary skills.

OVERHEAD CAST WITH OPEN FACE SPINNING REEL

1

Grip the rod and reel as shown. With free hand rotate reel's cowling until line roller is beneath extended index finger. Pick up line with that finger and flop open bail with other hand.

10 o'clock

2

Stand with body angled slightly toward target. Center the rod with tip top at eye level (10 o'clock). Position elbow close to your side; your forearm in line with the rod.

stop at 1 o'clock

stroke

drift

3

Begin by swiftly raising head almost to eye level, pivoting elbow.

4

When the rod reaches 1 o'clock, the weight of the bait will cause it to bend to rear. At this time bring rod forward in a crisp downstroke.

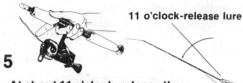

11 o'clock-release lure

5

At about 11 o'clock, release the finger holding line. If bait goes straight up, you released too soon; if it plops in front of you, you released too late.

6

As your bait nears target, gently "feather" line with index finger. The moment it hits target, place index finger on edge of spool to stop flight of bait and prevent slack build-up on reel spool.

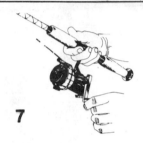

7

Without changing hands, begin retrieve. The line guide will automatically flop over.

PLAYING AND LANDING A FISH

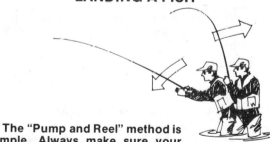

The "Pump and Reel" method is simple. Always make sure your line is tight. Raise your rod tip and as you drop it, reel the line in. Repeat this until you can grab or net the fish.

BASIC
PRINCIPLES OF SURF CASTING

1) In casting with a spinning surf rod and reel, hold the rod with the right hand at the reel seat with the thumb on top and other fingers below. Two fingers can be in front of the leg or support of the reel, and two behind. Left hand holds the rod butt. With a full bail pick-up, turn the reel handle with your left hand until the line roller is on top; then pick up the line with the index finger of the right hand. Then back off the reel handle so that the line is freed from the roller, after which the left hand pushes the wire bail down until it locks in the casting position. Bring the rod up to shoulder height with the reel facing up as shown in the first drawing.

2) Next, with a quick motion, bring the rod tip up over your head.

3) and 4) The tip will bend in an arc and then start to propel the bait forward, at which time you release the line from your finger and bring the rod down with the tip pointing toward the target. When the bait reaches the spot, bring your finger down to the lip of the spool to stop the cast. Timing is the most important factor in casting, along with the "feel" of the weight of the lure or sinker.

4
FISH IDENTIFICATION

The main difference between fresh and saltwater fish is size. In some cases, you will find the same species available in both environments. All rivers eventually drain into the sea. There comes a point in the flow when fresh and salt water meet. Known as **brackish water,** these areas can be home to many species found in rivers and reservoirs such as the black bass family, catfish, perch and striped bass.

Fish occupy all levels of **inshore waters**, with the majority found close to the bottom. These species will also seek out structure, like their river brethern, to protect them from the force of tidal changes, but allow them to feed. Others known as **pelagic** species, will work the middepths and surface in search of whatever bait happens to be around.

Fish are a product of their environment. Normally, their physical characteristics will indicate their lifestyle. Most pelagic species have streamlined bodies, while their bottom seeking counterparts will be proportionately heavier in build. Species who take up residence around reefs and rocks will have heavier bodies and broader tails that are designed to allow them to maneuver in this environment.

The drawings on the following pages only begin to identify the many species found in inshore salt water in this country.

ATLANTIC COAST & GULF

BLACK DRUM

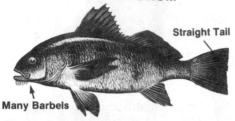

Straight Tail

Many Barbels

Avg. Wgt. 40 lbs.

BLACKFISH (TAUTOG)

Avg. Wgt. 2-3 lbs.

BLUEFISH

Short Dorsal Spines

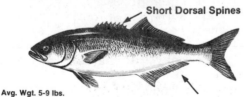

Avg. Wgt. 5-9 lbs.

Long Anal Fin

BONEFISH

Blackish

Avg. Wgt. 5-6 lbs.

CHANNEL BASS

Prominent Black Spot

No Barbels

Avg. Wgt. 25 lbs.

FLOUNDER (FLUKE)

Large Mouth

Eyes on Left Side

Avg. Wt. 1-3 lbs.

GRAY MANGROVE SNAPPER

Dark Stripe

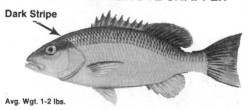

Avg. Wgt. 1-2 lbs.

FLORIDA POMPANO

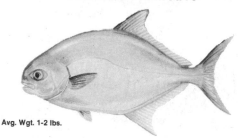

Avg. Wgt. 1-2 lbs.

SHEEPSHEAD

Avg. Wgt. 3 lbs.

SNOOK

Black
Lateral Line

Avg. Wt. 11 lbs.

STRIPED BASS

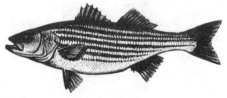

Avg. Wgt. 2-5 lbs.

WEAKFISH AND
SPOTTED SEATROUT

Round Black Spots

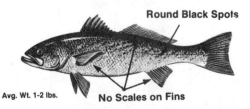

Avg. Wt. 1-2 lbs.

No Scales on Fins

WHITING (KINGFISH)

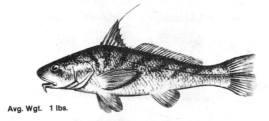

Avg. Wgt. 1 lbs.

PACIFIC COAST

BARRED SAND BASS

3rd Spine Longest

Dark Bars

Avg. Wgt. 3½ lbs.

BARRED SURFPERCH

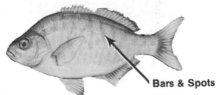

Bars & Spots

Avg. Wgt. 1-2 lbs.

CALIFORNIA CORBINA

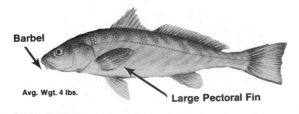

Barbel

Avg. Wgt. 4 lbs.

Large Pectoral Fin

JACKSMELT

Avg. Wgt. 1 lb.

KELP BASS

Pale Spots

Avg. Wgt. 3-4 lbs.

LINGCOD

Avg. Wgt. 4-5 lbs.

OPALEYE

Blue-Green

Pale Spots

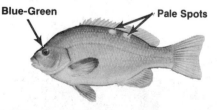

Avg. Wgt. 2 lbs.

PACIFIC HALIBUT

Avg. Wgt. 50-400 lbs.

COPPER ROCKFISH
(OVER 60 SPECIES OF ROCKFISH)

Pale Strip

Avg. Wgt. 2-3 lbs.

SARGO

Dark Bar

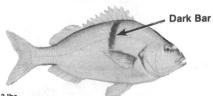

Avg. Wgt. 2-3 lbs.

STARRY FLOUNDER

Black Bands on Fins

Yellow Bands on Fins

Avg. Wgt. 4-5 lbs.

EXTERIOR FEATURES
SOFT-RAYED FISH

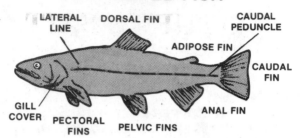

LATERAL LINE

DORSAL FIN

CAUDAL PEDUNCLE

ADIPOSE FIN

CAUDAL FIN

GILL COVER

PECTORAL FINS

PELVIC FINS

ANAL FIN

SPINY-RAYED FISH

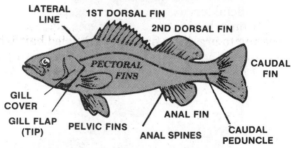

LATERAL LINE

1ST DORSAL FIN

2ND DORSAL FIN

CAUDAL FIN

PECTORAL FINS

GILL COVER

GILL FLAP (TIP)

PELVIC FINS

ANAL FIN

ANAL SPINES

CAUDAL PEDUNCLE

INTERIOR FEATURES

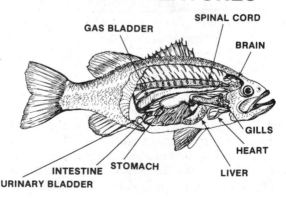

GAS BLADDER

SPINAL CORD

BRAIN

GILLS

HEART

LIVER

INTESTINE

STOMACH

URINARY BLADDER

5

NATURAL BAIT
AND HOW TO RIG IT

Inshore saltwater fishing is almost exclusively **natural** bait fishing, especially for the beginner. At one time, all natural bait was **alive**. However, many times it will come to the fisherman in a frozen form, such as squid, or the fisherman will dissect it himself.

Artificial lures are normally relegated to trolling from a boat, some surf fishing, jigging and casting to breaking fish after schooled baitfish on the surface. As in many freshwater fishing situations, sometimes the two kinds of bait are mixed together into some of the most amazing looking contraptions you can imagine. As in all fishing, you are only limited to your imagination. When in doubt, experiment.

Great care should be taken in caring for your bait. Most tackle shops keep the supply they sell you in a refrigerator. If you plan to do the same, it's a good idea to check with the woman of the house before you do it. Some people have a hard time with a box of worms, crabs or clams sitting next to tonight's dinner.

The rigs you use to catch your quarry normally revolve around the **bottom rig**. With a change in sinker styles, this rig may also be used in **drift fishing**. You can make them yourself, but be advised that they don't cost much and it's much easier to buy them at the local tackle shop. The following outlines the proper rigging for popular natural baits.

CUT BAIT

CUT STRIP
FOR DRIFT FISHING

CHUNK STRIP
FOR BOTTOM FISHING

Cut bait can come from any fish available. In salt water it is better to use fish with an oily, tough skin.

1. With a sharp knife and cutting board slice fillets from both sides of the fish and throw the rest away.

2. If you are drift fishing, cut narrow strips and run your hook through one end of one of the pieces.

3. If you are bottom fishing, the chunk should be more squarish. Run the point of your hook through this piece at least twice.

BLOODWORMS AND CLAMWORMS

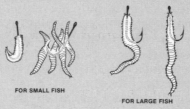

FOR SMALL FISH

FOR LARGE FISH

These worms make great baits for many saltwater fish. Believe it or not, bloodworms actually bleed when you cut them in half.

Put them on your hook as shown above. Thread part of the worm on your hook, the way you do with earthworms, for small fish. Use whole worms for large fish.

ANCHOVIES

For the best action from an anchovy, hook it through the nose (ahead of the eyes). The nose is the toughest portion of this delicate bait. Another popular method that is especially effective when bottom fishing is collar hooking. This is demonstrated in the righthand illustration.

SHRIMP

HOOKING
LIVE SHRIMP

HOOKING
-DEAD SHRIMP

It is important for the shrimp to move around when you cast them into the water. So, it's important for it to be alive and unless you hook it properly, it won't be. There is a dark spot on the head behind the snout. Put your hook through the dark spot and you will kill the shrimp. If you head hook the bait, do it away from this spot.

The other way to hook a shrimp is to thread it onto your hook. Run your hook from the underside of the tail, through the entire tail and out behind the head.

If the shrimp is dead, run the hook from the underside of the tail, through the tail and out the belly of the shrimp.

FIDDLER CRAB

REMOVE
CLAW

The fiddler crab is available in many tidal areas of the United States. The first thing you do with a fiddler is remove its large claw. This is because if you don't, the crab will grab onto an object in the water and won't move the way you want him to. Now insert your hook into the claw hole and thread the bend of the hook until you can push the point of the hook out through its side.

MOLE CRAB
(Sand Flea, Sandbug, Sand Crab and Scud)

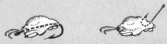

This is an excellent surf bait. Hook it from underside rear and out the back or hook between the antennae and push the hook through the center of the body and out the back with the point of the hook pointed downward.

CRAB

PEELER CRAB (Shedder)

REMOVE OUTER SHELL	**CUT INTO VARIOUS SIZE PARTS**	**CONCEAL HOOK**

SOFT CRAB

USE HALF FOR LARGER FISH   **HOOK THE SAME AS PEELER FOR SMALL FISH**

HARD CRAB

  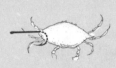

REMOVE CLAWS

The blue crab goes through several stages in its life. At a certain time of year the crab will begin to lose its shell. At this time it is called a "peeler crab" in some parts of the country. Then, it will lose its shell altogether. This is a "softcrab". After it grows its shell back it's a "hard crab".

CLAMS

There are many kinds of clams that may be used for bait. The sea clam is very popular on the Atlantic Coast, especially in chumming. Frozen sea clam is cut ready for the hook. Both the soft belly and tougher snout sections can be used from Manoe clams, if they are available.

BAITFISH

There are 3 basic ways to hook live baitfish:

1) Through the back, missing the spin. Usually the hook is inserted in the middle of the back. However, if you want it to look up-hook it closer to the head and if you want the bait to swim downwards-closer to the tail.

2) Fragile baitfish should be hooked through the eye sockets.

3) Through both lips when fishing in strong currents.

SQUID

There are numerous species of squid found along the Atlantic and Pacific coasts. Squid do not keep well and usually come to the fisherman frozen. Most often large squid are fished whole for offshore species. However, smaller whole squid can be hooked as shown above on an 3/0 hook (s) and bottom fished or drifted for larger inshore species.

Portions of the body are also effective. Normally the squid is cut into triangles big enough to cover the hook.

SALTWATER RIGS

FISH FINDER RIG

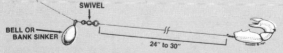

May be used for drifting or bottom fishing. This rig allows the fish to take your bait without feeling the resistance of the sinker. It also gives live bait the ability to move around if your reel is in free-spool.

DOUBLE BOTTOM AND DRIFT RIGS

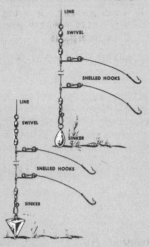

Normally used for smaller species of fish. When fishing from a location where the rig should hold to the bottom, use a pyramid type sinker. If you are drift fishing from a boat, use a rounded type sinker that won't get hung up.

SPREADER RIG

Another drift rig. Best to use this rig when drifting in murky water that doesn't allow good visibility.

CHUMMING RIG

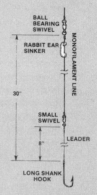

The secret in this rig is the weight of your sinker.

SURF RIG

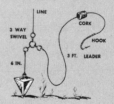

In surf fishing, always use a pyramid type sinker. The size you chose will depend on the current. Also, a float (cork) will help keep crabs off your bait.

HOOK SELECTION

There is no fixed rule on hook selection and size. Saltwater species are more inclined to a wider range in size than their freshwater counterparts.

ATLANTIC COAST & GULF OF MEXICO

HOOK SIZE	SPECIES
3/0 - 7/0	Black Drum
#4 - 2/0	Blackfish (Tautog)
3/0 - 7/0	Bluefish
#1 - 2/0	Bonefish
5/0 - 9/0	Channel Bass (Red Drum, Redfish)
#8 - #2	Founder (Fluke)
#4 - 4/0	Mangrove Snapper
1/0 - 2/0	Pampano
1/0 - 4/0	Sheepshead
4/0 - 6/0	Snook
1/0 - 6/0	Striped Bass (Striper, Rockfish)
#1 - 5/0	Weakfish & Spotted Sea Trout
1/0 - 3/0	Whiting (Kingfish)

PACIFIC COAST

HOOK SIZE	SPECIES
#4 - 3/0	Barred Sand Bass
#8 - #1	Barred Surfperch
#6 - #1	California Corbina
#8 - #2	Jacksmelt
#4 - 3/0	Kelp Bass (Calico Bass)
1/0 - 6/0	Lingcod
#8 - #4	Opaleye
#6 - 3/0	Pacific Halibut
#1 - 5/0	Rockfish (Over 60 Species)
#8 - #1	Sargo
#8 - #1	Starry Flounder

6
ARTIFICIAL BAITS

The basic difference between artificial baits used in landlocked reservoirs, flowing rivers and saltwater bays, is size. Although, at first glance, there may appear to be a more pronounced difference in the artificials used in offshore fishing endeavors, these lures, in the majority, are only large, fancy versions of the freshwater jig. The major difference being that the offshore version has a hollow metal head and is meant to be fished on the surface as it is trolled behind a fast moving boat.

Trolling is a technique employed by many freshwater anglers. By dragging your offering behind a boat, a lot of territory can be covered in search of your quarry. This technique takes on new meaning in salt water. Saltwater species generally fall into one of two catagories. The **pelagic** group is equipped with streamlined bodies and spend most of their time at mid-depths in search of baitfish while the other group is content working the **bottom depths**. The pelagic group is the normal prey of the trolling angler, although some bottom species are also effectively taken in this manner.

On the following pages you will see many lures that are very familar if you do any reservoir or river angling. You will also be introduced to jigs that look like metal minnows or larger versions of their freshwater counterparts, surgical tubing lures made from materials used in hospitals and very large spoons.

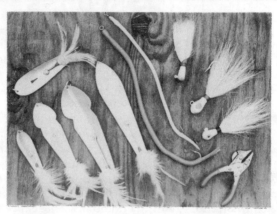

Trolling Lures: on the left-saltwater spoons; in the middle-surgical hose; on the right-saltwater jigs.

It is important that your surgical hose have a twist in the lower half of the lure. If not, it will not rotate in the water which duplicates the swimming motion of an eel.

TROLLING SPOONS

In many coastal parts of the country, the **saltwater spoon** is the premier trolling artificial bait. Similar in design to many of the freshwater spoons, the saltwater version ranges in size all the way up to 8 inches and is usually sparsely dressed with feathers.

The action of a large spoon in the water, when trolled, is amazing. When the boat is moving slowly, it can swing a full 4 feet to either side of its line of travel.

Care must be taken when rigging this lure because their erratic action can cause severe line twists. A ball bearing snap swivel, attached to the leader of the weight to take it down to the desired depth, is a must. An additional barrel swivel somewhere in the leader, is a good backup.

Spoons must be trolled at the correct speed to be effective. A good indicator is your rod tip. When your boat is traveling at the correct speed, the lure will move from side to side, put additional pressure on the rod, and cause the rod tip to bounce or **tick** very rapidly. That's a sign your lure is performing as it should.

SURGICAL TUBING

The saltwater equivalent to the plastic worm is an eel imitation sometimes referred to as **surgical tubing** or **hose**. These lures are rigged with wire connecting the swivel to a single or double hook at the end. A length of surgical tubing covers the rig and the lure is given a **slight twist** in the lower half to make it rotate through the water. This motion, when viewed from the side, duplicates the swimming motion of an eel. Some rigs use **bead chain**, a heavy version of the chain

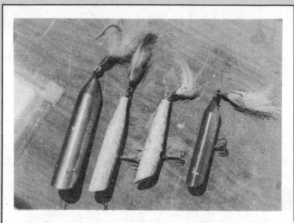

Saltwater surface plugs are similar to freshwater surface plugs. The main difference is size and construction.

Examples of trolling lures. The broken back lure is meant to represent an injured baitfish.

used in many key chains or a swivel in the center to give the lure a **broken back** effect and some styles are made with a lead head. As with spoons, the same precautions should be taken to prevent line twists.

TROLLING LURES

A larger version of the freshwater crankbait, these lures come with different size lips that will take them to various depths when trolled. Normally, no sinker systems are required. All the angler has to do is let out 50' to 150' of line and the lure will take care of the rest.

As with any lure with a wobbling action, attach this bait to a heavy plain snap.

SURFACE LURES

A bigger, heavier version of the freshwater surface lure, these baits are reserved for breaking fish. When you come across breaking fish, the action is fast and normally only lasts a few minutes. For this reason, many anglers prefer to remove the **treble** hooks in favor of single ones for ease of hook removal.

When you find a school of breaking fish, cast your plug out and retrieve it as fast as you can. Don't worry about the speed of your retrieve, it can't be too fast. In fact, chances are you might hook and lose several fish, all on the same cast.

DIVING LURES

A lot of inshore saltwater fishing will revolve around fishing near **structural clements** such as old piers, duck blinds and channel markers. As the fish in these areas are trying to escape the force of tidal changes and strong currents, it is necessary to get your offering down to them. These situations are ideal for casting lures, among others.

There are many of these lures on the market

Jigs may be trolled or jigged off the bottom.

today. Normally they are big versions of the diving lures used in fresh water. Many come with plastic lips. But, the lures outfitted with metal lips have the advantage of allowing you to change the angle of the lip by bending it and thus varying its diving effect.

JIGS

The saltwater jig has **two** basic functions.

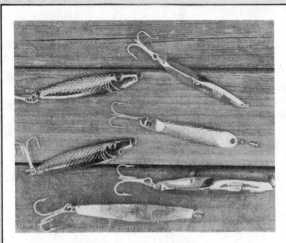

Examples of jigs. Notice how they resemble minnows. Normally fished in deep water after fish are located there, the idea is to jig them off the bottom.

Depending on size, this lure may be **jigged** off the bottom for the species of fish who prefer this part of a saltwater bay, or they may be **trolled** behind a moving boat, which will be explained in Chapter 11.

Three types of dressing are primarily used on saltwater jigs. They are **bucktail** (deer tail), **feathers** or **twister tails**. Although there are no hard and fast rules regarding their use, feathers are often preferred on smaller jigs (1/0-4/0), and bucktail is used on the larger, trolling jigs (up to 8/0). Twister tails are effective on most all sizes and many times you will find jigs tipped with strips of **pork rind**, or **cut bait**.

Large jigs are usually trolled one to a line. The small size, however, are often trolled together in a **daisy chain** or **umbrella rig.** This technique is meant to represent a school of baitfish.

Always tie a single jig directly to your line. They will run true and not cause any line twist.

Jigs are sold by hook size or weight, sometimes both. In general, match the hook size to the species of fish available in trolling situations, and be less concerned with the weight. The rig the jig is used with will take care of that.

Jigs completes the discussion on saltwater lures. Be assured that, depending on the part of the country you live in, there will be variations on the various lures discussed in this chapter. But, upon a closer examination, you will probably find that the local interpretation is not really that different.

LEADER

Long by freshwater standards, saltwater trolling leader can be up to 40' in length. Leader strength can be the same as the line on your reel. However, sharp toothed fish can make you feel more comfortable with leader that is 20 or even 30 pound test heavier.

Obviously, you can only reel your line in to the beginning of the leader. So, if you are using leader **under** 50 pound test, it is advisable to have a pair of heavy cotton gloves on board to protect your hands against cuts as you pull it in.

7

MARINE ELECTRONICS

I f electronics are important to the freshwater angler, they're nothing short of critical to his saltwater counterpart. Not only do these electronic gems help locate fish, but in some cases, are even responsible for many a boating fisherman's life being saved.

A good set of charts and at least a **flasher depthfinder** should be mandatory equipment on any boat, be it power or sail. Since saltwater boats are normally many times the size of most reservoir rigs, they **draw** a lot more water with their deep V hulls and thus are subject to running aground in shallow areas. If the captain pays attention to his charts and depthfinder, normally this unhappy fate can be avoided.

A **VHF** radio is also a very important tool to have aboard. A CB radio might be fine to gossip with your pals, but it is the VHF that has the range to call **for help** in an emergency.

LORAN is a navigational device that reads crossing radio frequencies. With the aid of charts that are designed to be used with this equipment, an angler can identify his position on the water and be assured that he is within 50 feet of the location indicated on the chart. This can be important if you have located underwater structure that holds fish, such as a ledge or dropoff. With this equipment, you can return to the same area, again and again.

DEPTHFINDERS AND CHART RECORDERS

After the knotted line and weight of Mark Twain's day, the first commercial electronic depthfinders were called **flashers**. These machines had a small light that rotated rapidly around a dial and indicated water depths. With practice, it was possible to determine bottom type and structure that was present in the area.

A new version of the old flasher. This one has an alarm system.

Technology didn't stop here. Soon **flasher-graphs** were available. Relying on the same technology as the flasher, these units printed out on paper what the flasher saw. They, however, weren't very accurate.

An example of new video systems on the market.

Next came the **straight line chart recorders**. Many feel these units are the best available. Most print out on paper, but video models are available.

An example of an LCD unit.

Recently, **LCD** units have hit the market. Displaying pictures on their screens using technology similar to a digital watch, one of the main advantages of these units is the ease of seeing the picture in bright sunlight.

One of new LORAN units.

With all these units, you get what you pay for.

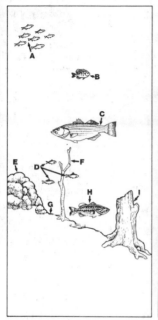 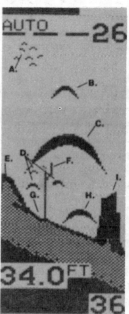

An artist's rendering of what an LCD is portraying on the right. The area shown is from 26' to 36'. The bottom slope runs from 32' to 34'. Thus, the total range covered is 26' to 36', with the bottom depth at 34'. Each dot represents ½" in height on the LCD screen.

A. School of Minnows
B. Small Fish
C. Large Fish
D. Minnows
E. Rocks
F. Small Tree
G. Bottom Slope
H. Medium Fish
I. Tree Stump

A typical VHF radio. Although it looks like a CB, it is really a telephone.

An example of a transducer. This is the other half of your depthfinder, recorder or LCG. It fits to the hull of your boat and sends and receives the signal that is translated on the screen of your unit. Always make sure the transducer you buy is designed for your total unit.

SURFACE THERMOMETER

The **surface thermometer** is a very useful item to have in brackish water fishing. With the addition of the tide, bass will seek structure and many times will be covered so that they won't show up on your depthfinder or recorder. So, what you are doing with this equipment is trying to locate this underwater structure and that is where the surface gauge comes into the picture. If it is springtime, you will be looking for warmer patches of structure infested waters. If is is a hot summer day, you will be looking for cooler areas.

VHF RADIO

These radio systems are very similar to the telephone you have at home. With the aid of a **marine operator**, you can call anyplace in the world, if you wish. There are a number of channels on these radios and many times they are used like CB radios. The main difference is their **superior** range.

OTHER GEAR

Most larger boats, and many reservoir rigs with built-in gas tanks, will have safety gear aboard. A lot of these boats have **electric bilge pumps** that will pump water out of your boat when it reaches a certain level. Another important safety item for inboard motors is a **fume detector**. This device will signal an alarm if gas fumes are present in your bilge. This is important because it only takes one spark to start a serious fire.

Even though it is not considered electronics, it goes without sayng that a properly serviced **fire extinguisher** should be aboard all gas powered boats.

Last, but not least, is a good **compass**. Without this piece of equipment it is pretty hard to make use of your charts.

8

TIDES AND CURRENTS

In most of the saltwater places people fish there is a **high tide** and, approximately 6 hours later, a **low tide.** The major element that controls the rise and fall of the tides is the position of the moon and sun in relation to the earth with the moon exerting the most influence. Since the moon rises about 50 minutes later each 24 hour period, you can normally count on a tidal change one hour later the next day.

To further confuse the issue, the stage of the moon the earth is experiencing will effect how high or low the tides will be. During **spring tides**, which occur during a new or full moon, you can expect an above average rise and fall of the tides and usually very good fishing conditions. Between the new and full moon, when the moon is in its partial phases, the tides will be more uniform and usually fishing isn't as good. These are called **neap** tides.

Tidal change and the currents they create are probably the most important factors in saltwater fishing. Fish move from one area to another mainly for feeding purposes. However, it is important that they stay in water that agrees with their cold blooded bodies. Even in relatively restricted waters, a tidal change can cause severe temperature changes, not to mention flood areas with food.

High tide occurs when an incoming tide

A portion of a tidal area at low tide. When the high tide comes in these areas will be completely flooded.

KEY WEST, FLA., 1988

Times and Heights of High and Low Waters

FEBRUARY

Day	Time h m	Height ft	m	Day	Time h m	Height ft	m
1 M	0318	-0.3	-0.1	16 Tu	0249	-0.6	-0.2
	0951	0.8	0.2		0928	0.9	0.3
	1414	0.3	0.1		1359	0.1	0.0
	2103	1.7	0.5		2054	2.0	0.6
2 Tu	0351	-0.3	-0.1	17 W	0328	-0.6	-0.2
	1015	0.9	0.3		1001	1.1	0.3
	1456	0.2	0.1		1458	-0.1	0.0
	2141	1.7	0.5		2146	1.9	0.6

A portion of a tide table put out each year by the government.

reaches its crest, and the outgoing tide occurs when it reaches its maximum retreat. The tide is called a **flood tide** on the way in, a **half tide** midway during this 6 hour period and **half slack water** when it reaches its peak. An **ebb tide** occurs when the water reverses itself and is known as **low slack water** at the end of this process. **Dead water** occurs at the very end of high and low tide. At this time, the water seems to come to a complete stop. This, however, is not always the case.

Many coastal bays empty out through inlets. In some cases the narrow inlet impedes the flow of the outgoing water to such an extent that this ebbing is taking place long after the tidal change and the incoming current meets the outgoing water and creates some pretty **dangerous** conditions.

Due to the varying conditions in saltwater fishing areas, there is no phase of the tide that results in the best fishing. However, most surf fishermen would probably agree that a flood tide offers the best overall chance for catching fish. This is especially true at night and early morning. The reason these anglers would pick the flood tide is because this incoming water is churning up all the sea creatures that fish feed on and depositing them in areas that are easier for the surf angler to cast too.

In some cases slack water provides the best fishing. This would be especially true around **reefs** and some **wrecks** where the tidal current is too strong during the periods of heavy movement for fish to venture out in search of food.

Tidal currents are a direct result of tidal changes. When 2 tides meet, it is called a **tidal rip**. During the slack period of the tide,

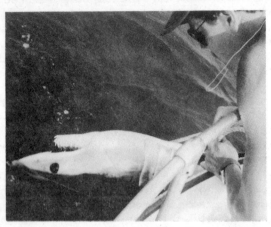

Tidal currents have very little effect on fishing far offshore. This deep water angling is influenced by oceanic currents instead.

Care should be taken when navigating a coastal inlet. This is especially true in a narrow inlet. The flow of outgoing water is impeded to such an extent that this ebbing is still taking place while the incoming tide is entering the inlet. These conditions can be dangerous to navigate.

you can count on baitfish keeping close to the beach and bars out of harms way. During strong flood and ebb tide currents, these same baitfish are washed into channels of bays where fine fishing takes place, especially during the first 2 hours of the flood or ebb tide.

All coastal areas have a tide table that will tell fishermen and boaters when to expect the high and low tides each day. Produced by the **National Oceanic and Atmospheric Administration**, these tables use various reporting stations on both coasts and the Gulf of Mexico to base these predictions on. Don't think that just because the table that covers your areas says that the first high tide for the day is at 9:39 AM, it will happen at that time in the particular area you happen to be. Each tide table is further broken down with **tidal variations**. These variations could be as much as 4 hours different, in some cases. It is important that you know the variation for your area and figure it into the tidal predictions.

Other elements are also responsible for tidal conditions and their effect on fishing. **Barometric pressure**, which will reverse itself before and after a storm, has a positive effect. Just before and after a storm are normally excellent times to fish.

Wind is also very important to understand tides and currents. It also can be responsible for blowing warm or cold waters in or out from coastal areas and thus, has a direct bearing on the quality of fishing.

As stated earlier, tides and currents are probably the most important influences on saltwater fishing. They play a major role in the life style of fish and the baitfish they feed on.

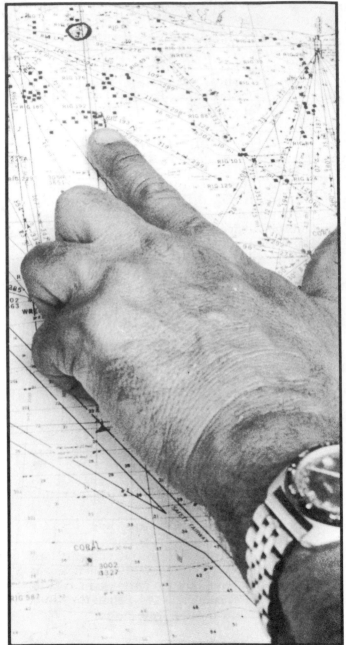

9

READING COASTAL CHARTS

The fisherman who knows how to read a **coastal** chart and find his position will not only have a safer trip, but find areas that hold fish. As we have learned, most bottom feeding fish will seek out structure to protect them from the force of a tidal change and still allow them to feed. The map will identify these areas and many times show you shore features and water markers you can use to navigate.

The best charts for saltwater fishermen are the **Small Craft (SC) Charts** produced by the **National Oceanic and Atmospheric Administration (NOAA)**. With depth findings in feet, all charts reflect measurements at **low tide**. This means the areas shown should not get any shallower and may be higher, depending on the stage of the tide.

The following is a section of one of these charts for Barnegat Bay in New Jersey. Take time to become familar with the buoys and other water markers and how they are represented on these charts. If you understand the explanation that follows, you will be able to read most Small Craft Charts and identify likely holding areas for fish.

In some bays, tidal flows, especially at low water, will allow you to view areas your charts will describe. But, in most parts of a bay your only help will come from these charts which are available at most marine stores.

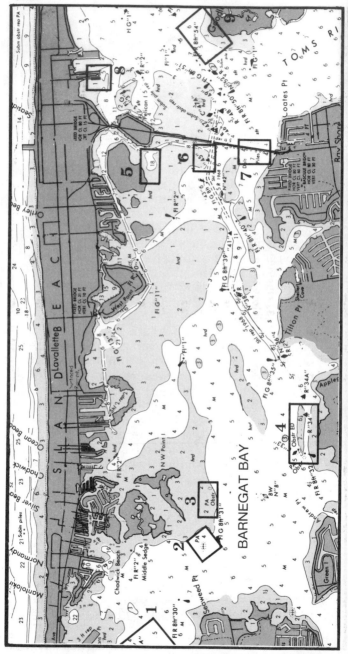

REFER TO MAP ABOVE

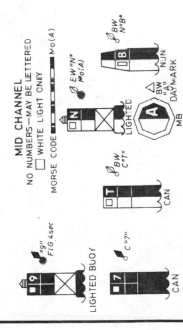

MID CHANNEL
NO NUMBERS—MAY BE LETTERED
☐ WHITE LIGHT ONLY
MORSE CODE ●○(A)

LIGHTED BUOY

"9"
FLG.4sec

"7"
CAN

"7"
C

EW"N"
Mo(A)

BW
C"T"
CAN

N
LIGHTED

BW
"A"
DAYMARK

A
MB

BW
N"B"
NUN
B

1. A mid-channel marker. Deep water all around and may be passed on either side.

2. Submerged wreck. Probably good cover for fish. The map shows it is under 4 feet of water at low tide.

3. Obstruction. The map doesn't identify it, but being close to an edge, it could hold fish.

4. Buoys mark the channel. There's a long trough in the channel which could hold fish, but don't anchor in the channel!

5. Deep Hole. As the tide goes out, fish in shallow water would gather here.

6. A black "can" buoy #45. Structure on the edge of a channel is a good place to fish, and this one is easy to find.

7. Bridge pilings offer food and cover for the fish— a good bet.

8. Piers and docks can be productive spots. Cast under the pier and vary the depth of your retrieve.

9. Tides and currents sweep around this point. Fish the side that's protected from the tide— the fish will be waiting there for food carried by the current.

10

SHORE FISHING

If you live close enough to coastal or inland saltwater fishing areas, you are in for some fine fishing. These areas may be fished from shore, boats, piers, bridges and jetties. Here you will find a much wider variety of fish than you will in a reservoir or river. Most of them will be much larger.

Some of these fish will have been spawned thousands of miles away, while others might actually have been born in fresh water, only to venture into the ocean to grow up.

There are charter boats and party boats for hire that fish every day and know the best places to find fish. Also, there are marinas and boat liveries that will rent you a small rowboat and motor to fish the quiet back bays. Sometimes these places will also rent tackle.

Even when fishing from shore, it's a good idea for youngsters to wear a life jacket. You can never tell when they might slip and fall from a pier and remember, the sea has no mercy.

As has been stated before, most good saltwater fishing revolves around a tidal change, and this is especially true when fishing from a bridge, shore, rock pile or fishing pier. Try to plan your trip around a tidal change. It's also a good idea to be totally prepared. Chances are you will have a lot of gear to carry. It is a good idea to have a wagon or bucket to carry it in.

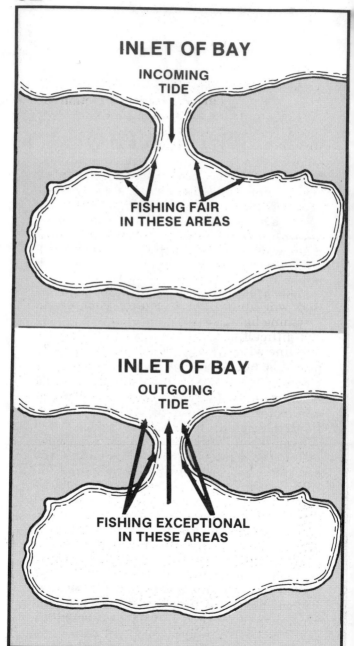

INLETS

The inlet to a bay is also a good place to fish. Always try to station yourself at the opposite corner of the inlet in relation to the direction the tide is traveling. So, if the inlet is experiencing an **incoming** tide, try to fish the corners of the inlet within the bay. On an **outgoing** tide do just the opposite. An **outgoing** tide almost always produces the best fishing because all the bait fish near the inlet will be washed out into the mouths of fish in wait.

BRIDGES

Whenever fishing in an area with a number of other fishermen, be it a party boat in the ocean, a pier at the beach or a bridge, it is advisable to have at least a medium action rod that will allow you to control your catch. Anything lighter would make controlling your fish difficult, which normally means a tangled line with your fellow anglers. Your line should be at least 15 pound test.

Unlike piers and jetties, bridges give you **more structural features** to choose from and thus, a greater assortment of gamefish to pursue. Since a bridge, especially a rather long one, passes over shoals, flats, underwater vegetation and channels, an angler can choose from bottom dwellers to the **pelagic** group, normally found chasing baitfish at mid-depth.

It is always tempting to cast your rig out as far as possible. However, when fishing natural bait on a bottom rig, this is normally not recommended for several good reasons. First of all, chances are you are a good way from water level. This will mean that you already have a good deal of line out just getting your rig to the bottom. The more line you let out, the harder it is to feel a bite. Secondly, the pilings

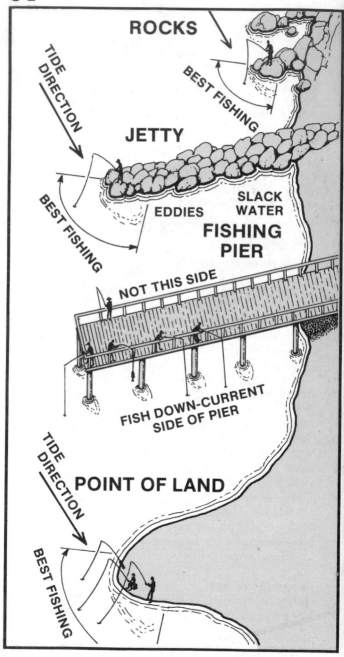

ROCKS

BEST FISHING

TIDE DIRECTION

JETTY

BEST FISHING

EDDIES

SLACK WATER

FISHING PIER

NOT THIS SIDE

FISH DOWN-CURRENT SIDE OF PIER

TIDE DIRECTION

POINT OF LAND

BEST FISHING

of the bridge can be a grocery store to many species. Attached to these pilings might be barnacles and don't forget small crabs and other marine life. Finally, many species of fish like the shade that a bridge and its pilings create.

Probably the best time to fish a bridge is at night. If possible, chose a spot near a street light that casts its glow on the water. Or, take a lantern and rope that can be lowered down to the water's surface. The light will attract baitfish, which in turn will attract the preditors you are after.

FISHING PIERS

The rule of thumb in pier fishing is the further you go out on the pier, the bigger the fish. Thus, a pier can be broken down into 3 distinct fishing areas.

The beach end, which is closest to the surf, will be very popular because you can expect to catch many bottom dwellers such as flounders, pompano and surfperch with your bottom rigs.

The middle section of the pier will produce the same species. Also, many anglers will fish with a float for species like weakfish.

The end of the pier will also produce what may be found in the middle pier area along with some of the larger fish, such as sharks.

Many piers have tackle shops that can give you updated information on what is working along with people to assist you. Normally these assistants have long handled gaffs to help you bring your catch over the rail.

THE SURF

Surf and jetty fishing are normally associated with coastal areas, although these angl-

Locating a slough can be as easy as finding an irregular wave pattern. If you find a stretch of beach with waves breaking at one point while others are breaking further out on both sides, you've found one.

ing situations are available in many bay areas. Although different in the size of equipment used and techniques employed, both rely on one basic element - the need for fish to protect themselves from strong direct currents.

To find the best surf fishing spots, walk the beach until you have identified areas with deep holes or irregularities on the bottom, within casting range. You can do this by studying the action of the waves. Since waves crest and break in shallow water, look for an area where the waves are breaking near the shore while on both sides they are breaking further from the beach. This indicates a trough or slough and is

In some areas of a bay, steep drop-offs will be within the reach of surf tackle and are excellent fishing areas from shore.

a gathering place for fish.

A sure sign of feeding fish will be circling sea birds that dive at the surface of the water to pick up pieces of baitfish left by a feeding school. When you see this happening, cast your lure or cut bait and retrieve your offering as close to the surface as possible.

Surf tackle is the largest spinning gear made. Two or three piece rods of 10 to 15 feet are the most popular. Reels should be able to hold at least 250 yards of 15 to 20 pounds test monofilament line. The bait you use is cut bait from an oily fish such as herring, menhaden, mackerel or squid.

Don't leave your bait on your hook for more than 30 minutes without changing it for a fresh chunk. Remember, fish are attracted by smell as well as sight.

Flat sided pyramid type sinkers of 2 to 5 ounces should be used if your rod can handle that much weight.

You may need more weight to hold the bottom if the current and tide are strong. Unless you plan on holding your rod and reel the entire time, a sand spike pushed into the beach is helpful.

It is important that your tackle be big enough to allow for a cast that will reach these troughs and sloughs. These areas are nothing more than indentations on the ocean's bottom that allow gamefish to avoid the power of the tide and current. If your tackle can't reach them, you are probably wasting your time.

Surf tackle is very specialized and expensive. Sometimes you can rent it from a local tackle shop.

Surf fishing in bays is a little different. Many

A hypothetical section of beach on either the Atlantic or Pacific coasts. Beach locations A, B and C are fishing locations and water areas 1,2,3, and 4 are areas that should hold fish under certain tidal conditions, be it high or low water.

Points 2 are right on top of the outer bar and should be fished most productively on a high tide. At this time marine creatures hunt these areas and will attract game fish looking for an easy meal. Depending on distance, these areas can be fished from the jetty (A) or the lower beach location (C). Don't pass them up!

Water point 4 is known as a "break". This is the area that game fish pass through and can be productive at any stage of high or low tide. Fish it from shore point B.

Water points 1 are sloughs, or deeper areas that should hold fish under most tidal conditions, and is easy to cast too.

Water point 3 is a "hole". This is the deepest water point on the drawing and should hold fish.

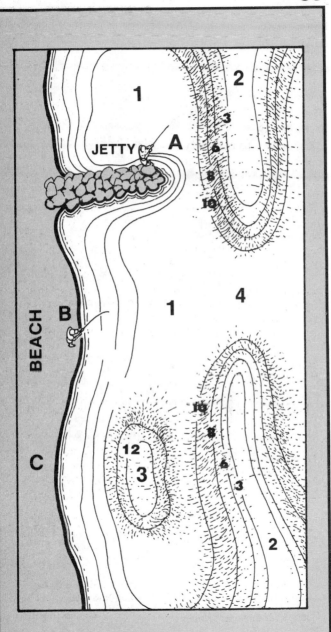

The striped bass was introduced to the West Coast in 1879. Though normally taken by boat anglers, some hit surf rigs occasionally!

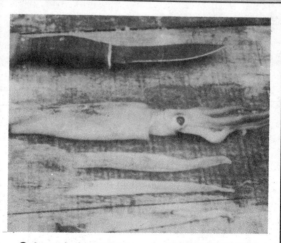

Cut or whole squid is a good saltwater bait for many situations, including surf fishing.

IMPORTANT

Most coastal communities are not very fond of surf fisherman. Normally resort communities, these cities and towns depend on vacationers for their very existence and feel that surf fisherman can create unnecessary hazards. For this reason most of these communities strictly regulate the hours, and in some cases, areas you may fish.

Fisherman, be they salt or freshwater oriented, have a tendency to be their own worst enemy. In many cases the problems anglers create for themselves revolve around policing the areas they fish, after they are through.

Never leave spent fishing line loose on the beach. Sea birds will get tangled up in it and in many cases, strangle to death.

Always bring in your line if there are swimmers in the area. The hook on your line is normally large enough and sharp enough to do real damage to a person.

Above all, exercise good common sense, and don't wreck it for the next guy!

shore areas in these waters that are accessible to the angler have steep dropoffs within reach of surf tackle. Fish will hang on these edges waiting for food to be washed down by the current.

JETTIES

Jetties are rock or concrete barriers, extending into a bay, inlet or ocean as protection against shoaling or erosion. Most were not built with fishermen in mind and navigating across them can be treacherous, especially when carrying an armful of tackle. Always wear shoes designed for wet, slippery surfaces along with waterproof clothing, if possible. You can be sure of one thing- you will get wet. In cool weather, it pays to be dry, if possible.

Generally, jetty fishing requires heavier rods in the 7 to 9' range and reels equipped with 14 to 20 pound monofilament line. Cut bait is a preferred method, but casting plugs are also used. Be sure to check with the local tackle shop about what artificial baits are working best. This is important because

Many times anglers will also fish jetties from a boat. Great care must be taken as this kind of fishing can be dangerous.

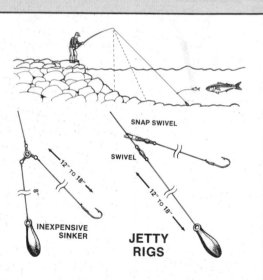

A couple of jetty live bait rigs you can make yourself. Don't spend a lot on these rigs because you will probably lose a couple in the rocks.

Jetties were not built with fishermen in mind. They can be very slippery.

Have a gaff at least 3 ft. long.

the species of fish found around jetties will vary, depending on your location.

The best time to fish a jetty is when the tide is flowing. This force of water drives baitfish in and out of the bay and gamefish will be in hot pursuit. Position yourself at the tip of the jetty on the far side where gamefish position themselves to avoid the force of the current so they can pick off an easy meal.

It is important to have a gaff with at least a 3 foot handle. After you have hooked and played a fish, you can be sure it will beach itself in the rocks.

As stated earlier, jetties can be very slippery. This can be especially true when they are wet and you must climb down rocks to gaff your catch or free a hung-up bait. Be careful, and above all, make a value judgement. If the breaking water looks too treacherous. Is the fish or bait worth the risk?

Saltwater fishing requires a great deal of common sense, not only to catch fish, but to be safe too.

11

BOAT
FISHING

Fishing from a boat is practiced using one of three different approaches; 1) while anchored; 2) while drifting with the current or 3) while trolling from a moving boat. All of the methods have there place and can be very effective. Many times the decision on the appropriate method will be determined by the underwater structural conditions in the immediate area, the species present, or local knowledge.

DRIFT FISHING

Drift fishing is the best way to explore most saltwater bays. In Chapter 9 we discussed saltwater charts. Different structural elements such as **ledges**, **submerged wrecks** and **holes** were identified. Obviously, it makes sense to try as **many** of these areas as possible to see if fish are present. That's what drift fishing is all about.

The direction of the tidal current normally dictates the direction of the drift, although high winds will sometimes be the determining factor. It makes sense to only drift over productive areas and this takes planning. If possible, plan your trip so that you can take advantage of an incoming and outgoing tidal change. Also, try to keep your fishing rig as **close** to the boat as possible. This way, with your bait almost straight down, it is easier to

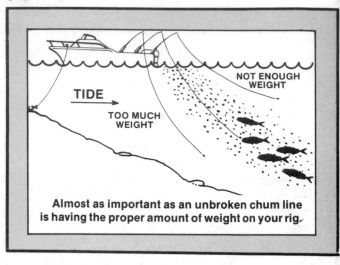

Almost as important as an unbroken chum line is having the proper amount of weight on your rig.

free a hung-up bait with a simple jerk of your rod tip.

In some cases, certain species of fish prefer that your offering be presented in a slow, steady fashion across the bottom. On the other hand, other fish, especially on the West coast, would rather attack a bouncing bait. This is accomplished by simply raising your rod tip.

Any of the drift rigs illustrated in Chapter 5 will work. It is important to use as **little** weight as possible with your rig.

BOTTOM FISHING
(STILL FISHING)

Bottom fishing requires that there be structure beneath you, in most cases. If, while drifting, you get a couple of good bites, chances are you have discovered an area that is worth your attention, and that is where bottom fishing comes in.

Normally the only difference between a bottom and drift rig is sinker selection. Most

Headboats (party) are found in most coastal areas and in many bay areas. For a small fee, you can go out and bottom fish or chum.

bottom rigs will employ a sinker that will hold the bottom, such as a pyramid type. Always try to anchor into the structure below and above all, keep your line taut. Short of a few species, it is advisable not to set the hook until you get a good tug on your line. If you are using a small live bait, set the hook immediately; if you are using a larger live bait, wait a second so your quarry can get the whole bait in its mouth.

If things slow down, its time to start **chumming**. Chum is ground up oily fish, clams or mussels that are slowly released over the side of the boat in a moving tide. This tactic creates a **slick** or **chum line**. It causes fish to school up and move towards the source. Use the rig illustrated in Chapter 5 and making sure you have the right amount of weight on your line. What happens is the fish follow the small pieces of bait towards their source until they reach the large piece on the end of your line. Make sure there are no breaks in your chum line or it won't work.

DILAPIDATED PIER

SUNKEN VESSEL

VISIBLE STRUCTURE

ARTIFICIAL REEFS

OUTSIDE BEND

DEEPER AREAS CAUSED BY SCOURING ACTION OF TIDAL CURRENT LIKELY TO HOLD MORE FISH

INSIDE BEND

CHANNEL

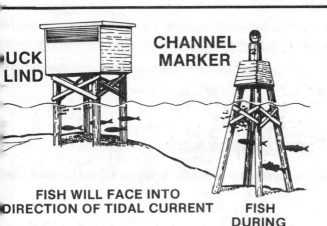

DUCK BLIND

CHANNEL MARKER

FISH WILL FACE INTO DIRECTION OF TIDAL CURRENT

FISH DURING SLACK TIDE

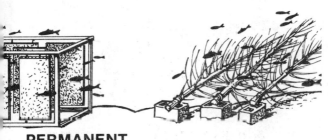

PERMANENT, MAN-MADE FISH ATTRACTORS

BELOW THE WATERLINE

DIRECTION OF CURRENT

SHELL BAR

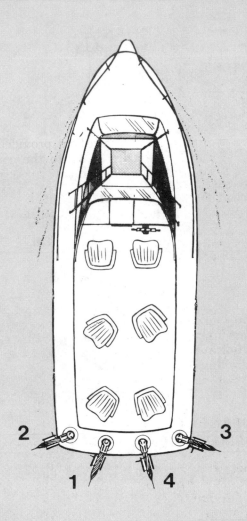

Many captains will fish 4 or more rods when trolling. A good plan for 4 rods is the illustration above. Rod #1 with 8 ounces of weight; rod #2 with 4 ounces of weight; rod #3 with 6 ounces of weight; and rod #4 with 10 ounces of weight.

TROLLING

Trolling is the best way to search for fish in a large body of water. The boat, moving at a **slow** speed, pulls a variety of lures through the water, usually at different depths, until fish are located.

You can troll from any size boat, provided the engine can be throttled down to the correct speed-**usually** 2 to 5 miles per hour. Sometimes the easiest way to accomplish this is to find a troller catching fish. Run beside him, at a distance, until you match his speed. When you have reached the correct speed, look at your rods and remember at what angle your line enters the water, or if your boat has a tachometer, note the R.P.M.'s it is showing. This technique can be misleading. The tachometer is measuring the **revolutions per minute** or how hard your engine is working. A boat going **into** a tide must work harder than one going **with** the tide and you will get two different readings.

Trolling rods are usually 20 to 30 pound class rods for most bay situations, however, 30 to 40 pound test line (one size heavier) is often used. The reel should have the capacity to hold 250 yards of line. **Conventional revolving spool reels** are best suited for trolling because the line comes straight off the reel without any line twists, and the **drag** mechanisms are of heavier construction, even though spinning reels are gaining in popularity.

Many times, experienced anglers will tell you to let out so many feet of line when fishing a particular depth or lure. The question is, how do you determine that you have let out that much line? One way is to use a **level wind** trolling reel. On **most** level wind reels, the vertical bars that the line passes through will let out

83

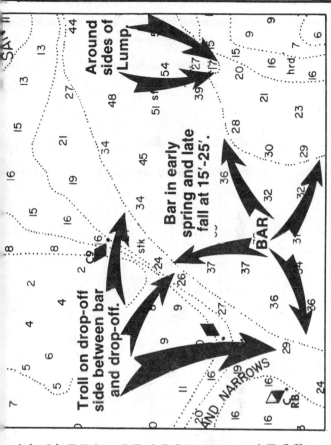

Around sides of Lump.

Troll on drop-off side between bar and drop-off.

Bar in early spring and late fall at 15'-25'.

BAR

The secret to successful trolling is finding areas with irregular bottom features such as dropoffs, edges and holes. These irregular bottom features will attract and hold bait fish. Feeding fish will seek these areas out for an easy meal.

If you have a chart of the area you plan on fishing, it's a good idea to study it before you go out. Mark off the areas that show an irregular bottom, such as the areas indicated on the map to the right. With the aid of your fish finder, they should not be too hard to locate when you are on the water.

Try and time your fishing activities within an hour of the tidal changes for that day. These times will normally produce the best fishing.

DROP SINKER RIG

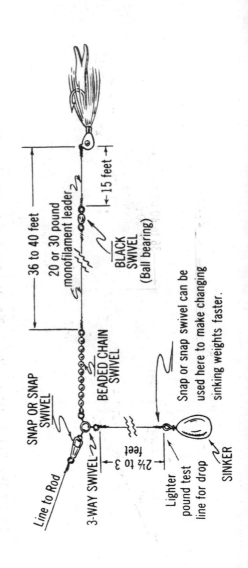

36 to 40 feet

15 feet

20 or 30 pound monofilament leader

BLACK SWIVEL (Ball bearing)

BEADED CHAIN SWIVEL

SNAP OR SNAP SWIVEL

Line to Rod

3-WAY SWIVEL

2½ to 3 feet

Snap or snap swivel can be used here to make changing sinking weights faster.

Lighter pound test line for drop

SINKER

IN-LINE SINKER RIG

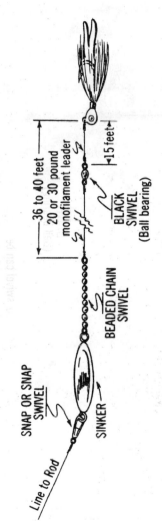

Line to Rod

SNAP OR SNAP SWIVEL

SINKER

BEADED CHAIN SWIVEL

36 to 40 feet
20 or 30 pound monofilament leader

BLACK SWIVEL (Ball bearing)

15 feet

The DROP SINKER RIG is a bottom trolling rig. If the depthfinder or recorder says they are on the bottom, this is the rig you would use. The IN-LINE SINKER RIG is used when the depthfinder or chart recorder tells you the fish are suspended (not on the bottom) in the water. This rig is not meant to take your bait or lure to the bottom.

The level wind is the vertical bars on the face of the reel. Every time it travels completely across the face of the reel, 10' of line is let out.

Jigging can be very effective around piers, bridge pilings and rock piles with any jig. Many times, cut bait is added. Fish will school within inches of the structure on a moving tide.

10 feet of line with each pass across the reel face.

Another time honored method of measuring line is to mark off 50 to 100 foot intervals with different color plastic tape. The only problem with this approach is that many times part of your line will break off. Then you must go through the procedure again which can prove tricky on a moving boat. If you are on your own, with no advice and only one rod, try letting out 100′ and adjust from there. If you are trolling more than one rod, let the other one out 150′ so that you can cover several depths. If someone hooks into a fish, it is always a good idea to reel in the other rods you are trolling to avoid line tangling.

JIGGING

If you are lucky enough to have a fishfinder (depthfinder or graph) on board your boat and happen to come across **schooled** fish suspended off the bottom, it's time for some jigging.

As illustrated in chapter 6, the saltwater jig can resemble a metal minnow or a large lead headed freshwater jig. The second variety may be trolled or jigged. When jigging, you might want to dress-up your offering with some cut bait. In either case, the idea is to locate the depth that the fish are holding and allow your bait to sink down to this level. Now, reel your line in a bit and then stop. What happens below is that the bait looks like it is trying to escape and then stops and dives for the bottom.

In a moving tide, try this technique around piers, bridge pilings and rock piles. The current will carry your jig to the fish's doorstep. You will probably lose some lures, but the results will make it worthwhile.

When the cooler waters of a bay drive fish into the shallows, you can feel them brushing against your boots. A quick retrieval of a surface lure should score.

Diving gulls are a sure sign of breaking fish and some lighter tackle plugging.

CASTING

Once in a while you will be lucky enough to encounter a school of breaking fish. A flock of diving gulls may point them out to you. What has happened is that a school of bait fish have surfaced and feeding predators, which are your quarry, are after an easy meal. As stated earlier, the action will be fast and furious, for a brief period of time. Tie on a surface plug, spoon, or shallow running plug and cast beyond the school and reel in as fast as you can. Don't worry about reeling-in too fast-you can't. It is not uncommon to hook and lose 2 or 3 fish before boating one, all on the same cast.

Casting is not necessarily limited to the above conditions. The visible structure illustration a few pages back can be effectively fished with the diving lures discussed in Chapter 6 or natural bait and a split shot sinker.

During the spring of the year, in many areas, water is much cooler in deeper depths. It is not uncommon in many bays to find **pelagic** species seeking warmer surface temperatures close to shore. At this time, tie on a **surface** or **shallow running lure**, cast it out and retrieve **quickly**. This technique works best on a **high** tide, but will work sometimes on a low tide. Just make sure the water is **moving** one way or the other.

IN CONCLUSION

Many techniques for catching fish have been discussed in this edition. Each has its place in the total scheme of fishing a saltwater bay. Being successful not only requires some knowledge, but a bit of **common sense**. This normally starts with good safety habits.

12

SAFETY

Safety around water starts with the clothing you wear. While ordinary clothing will suffice, it should be sturdy and serviceable. Because of the increasing dangers of skin cancer, it's a good idea to cover as much of your body as possible. Unless the fish you are after require camouflaged or dark clothing to conceal your presence, it normally is a good idea to wear light colored clothing to help reflect the sun. Always have a jacket or parka available.

Wearing a hat or cap is a good idea. In cold weather the addition of a hat will prevent the loss of body heat, while in warmer weather it will help guard against sunburn and assist in eliminating glare off the water.

Gloves are a good idea in cold weather. Although it might seem incompatible to wear gloves while fishing, the fact is that gloves are available which are pliable enough to allow you to tie knots and cast accurately.

Sun glasses are necessary outdoor gear. Not only do they protect against glare but shield your eyes against **ultaviolet** rays that many experts feel can damage them.

Insect repellents and sun blocks are also useful items to have with you. The best repellent is made from a substance called **DEET**. But, be aware that **DEET** will damage any plastic item. Great care must be taken when using this lotion since plastic is used in the construction of your tackle box, lures and parts of your reel. Sun block is necessary to prevent burning. **Number 15 or higher is recommended**.

Weather conditions should also be taken into consideration. **Lightening** can be very dangerous. This is especially true if you happen to be out in the middle of a saltwater bay during a lightening storm. If you get caught in one of these storms, get off the water as soon as possible. If you are trapped on the water, lay down all fishing rods and take down any radio antennas. Graphite rods are especially dangerous as graphite will attract lightening. Also, sit or lay on the deck of your boat so you are not an elevated target.

Even a peaceful bay can be dangerous in storms with **high wind** conditions. If you ever find yourself in severe wave conditions, face your boat, and ride into the waves until you can get off the water as soon as possible.

PFD'S, or personal flotation devices, are required when boating by the Coast Guard. The regulations generally require that there be one wearable PFD for **each** passenger and a throwable ring or cushion PFD for boats of a certain size or features. This safety gear is rated by type. Type I gear provides maximum flotation and will turn an unconscious person head and face up to prevent drowning. It is reversible for quick wearing and is available in adult and child sizes.

Type II PFD's will also turn the wearer to a vertical and slightly backward position to prevent the unconscious from drowning. They come in three sizes but do not give the long term protection and flotation that Type I does.

Type III PFD's are the type usually used by fishermen. They frequently have pockets and can double as fishing vests. They will maintain a face-up position, but will not turn an unconscious person to this position. Many sizes are available in both vest and jacket styles.

Type IV PFD's are designed to be grasped, not worn. They include flotation cushions and rings, and are designed to be thrown to a person who is overboard.

PFD's also help to maintain body heat in the water and help in preventing or minimizing hypothermia.

To prevent accidents and make boating enjoyable and safe, several rules of the road must be observed. An operator is considered in violation of boating laws if these are not followed. Negligent operation includes speeding, operating a boat in protected or swimming water or slow speed areas, skiing too close to swimmers or fishermen, causing waves to other boats or docking areas, taking the right away from a sailboat, running at night without lights and operating under the influence of alcohol. It is important that you are not only aware of these laws, but make sure that you practice them.

All fishermen should know how to swim. As you probably won't have a lifeguard available where you are fishing, try to follow the following precautions, if you decide to take a dip.

If you are by yourself **don't** go for a swim unless you fall overboard by accident. If you have a partner, make sure he or she is an **experienced** swimmer. It goes without saying if you have any doubts about your ability to swim, stay out of the water. Stay out of cold water, since hypothermia can result.

The word **hypothermia** has already been mentioned twice in this chapter. It's a good idea to understand exactly what hypothermia is and what to do if you encounter someone suffering from it.

Hypothermia is the chilling of a person **beyond** that person's **ability to rewarm** the body. If not corrected, chilling of the body core temperature causes weakness, hallucinations, uncontrollable limbs, and finally unconsciousness and death. Part of the body's protection is to sacrifice the blood flow and maintenance - of body heat in the limbs to protect and maintain body heat for the internal organs and brain.

One fallacy is that hypothermia can only occur in cold water. In fact, it can occur in almost **any temperature**, once the body begins to get cold or chilled through rain, wetting or wind.

To prevent hypothermia, dress warmly, carry spare clothing, keep your head warm, and use a waterproof parka or rain gear to protect against loss of body heat by rain and wind.

If you encounter someone who has succumbed to hypothermia, try to **secure professional medical help** as soon as possible. While waiting for this help or if no help is available, completely remove their wet or cold clothing and replace with warm clothing or place them in a warm bath. The administration of hot sweet drinks is approved, but **no alcoholic beverage** should be used. **Do not** warm the limbs and **do not exercise** the patient by walking. **Warming the limbs** will often cause increased blood flow to the limbs, resulting in **stroke, heart attack, and death**. In **extreme** cases, a warm bath, with the arms and legs outside of the bath water is ideal. A **good substitute** is a warm sleeping bag or electric blanket (only on the trunk, abdomen and head). Hypothermia is not a casual concern and each year many fishermen and other outdoorsmen die from it.

A person **overboard** can be a very serious situation. Many times it results in as much panic onboard as it does with the individual who fell overboard. It is **important** for all concerned to remain calm. The **throw-row-go** method of life saving is the recommended procedure to use to assist the individual in trouble.

The first safety procedure is to **throw** a life saving device to them. This should be a type IV PFD such as a ring or cushion, preferably attached to a rope. Lacking this, any floating object such as a cooler will help. If this is not possible, **row** a boat to the person, preferably with an assistant in the boat to help pull the person over the stern (rear) of the boat. If using a motor powered boat, the motor **must** be turned off before reaching the person overboard. If not, you run the risk of cutting the person with the motor prop. Do not allow the person overboard to try to pull themselves into a small boat over the side, since it might overturn your boat. Only an individual experienced in life saving should attempt to **go** into the water after the person. Drowning people will often panic and can hamper, injure or even drown their rescuer.

It goes without saying that **liquor and boating** don't mix. The heat of the sun, glare from the water and rocking of the boat only **increase** the intoxication process. Safe boating requires a clear mind and common sense. Being intoxicated **eliminates** proper usage of these abilities.

Knowledge of basic first aid is also essential on any fishing trip. Normally, you are in an area where medical care is unavailable and many times action should be taken before this help can be secured.

The most common medical problem that anglers face is the removal of a fish hook that has penetrated the skin beyond the barb. Usually it's a good idea to leave the removal to a professional if you can get to a medical facility in an hour or two. **In no case** should you ever attempt to remove a hook from around the eyes, the face, the back of a hand or from any area where ligaments, tendons or blood vessels are visible.

The simplist removal is to cut free the rest of the fishing lure and use a loop of heavy twine (heavy fishing line is satisfactory) around the bend of the hook. Next hold down the eye and shank of the hook, pressing it lightly into the skin. Grasp the loop and with a sharp jerk, pull the hook free. The downward pressure on the eye and shank of the hook clears the barb and allows it to travel out through the puncture wound. Be sure to have a **tetanus** shot as soon as possible unless such protection is already in effect.

Small cuts can be handled with antiseptic and bandages. Larger or deeper cuts require pressure directly on the wound to prevent excessive bleeding. To do this, use sterile, sealed gauze pads or as an alternative, an unfolded clean handkerchief. In the case of severe bleeding, in which an artery or vein has been cut, a tourniquet may be necessary as a last resort.

For cuts on arms and legs, the best direct pressure or tourniquet position is at the joint immediately above (closest to the body) the cut, where the major blood vessels travel over or near the bone. Use direct pressure here, or a properly applied tourniquet, to stem the flow of blood. In either case do not apply too much pressure, or pressure for too long. As soon as it is possible, call a doctor, get the individual to a hospital or call paramedics.

Fishing was never meant to be dangerous, just memorable. A comfortable, safe trip is far preferable to an uncomfortable, dangerous trip. Many times the difference revolves around a little common sense.

QUESTIONS TO ASK

If there is saltwater fishing within a reasonable distance from a tackle shop, you can bet they will stock saltwater gear. Many of these shops will also be able to give you current information on what species of fish are presently available in certain areas.

Obviously, it's always a good idea to find a tackle shop close to the area you plan to fish. He will specialize in the type fishing that produces in his area and have the right bait. Here are some questions to ask him.

1. Where is the best place around here to fish from shore?
2. What stage of the tide is best?
3. Do you have a corrected tide table I may have? If not, what is the correction for this area?
4. What live bait is producing and how is it being fished?
5. If your tackle isn't heavy enough, can you rent some?
6. I plan on doing some trolling. What artificial bait are the fish hitting and how deep are they?
7. What channel on the VHF is the marine operator? Does the Coast Guard monitor any channel?

REMEMBER, ALWAYS OBEY ALL SIZE MINIMUMS, THROW TRASH ONLY INTO A TRASH CAN OR BAG AND NEVER KEEP MORE FISH THAN YOU CAN USE.